CHINESE Favorites

fresh ❀ delicious ❀ easy

Publications International, Ltd.

Pictured on the front cover: Soy-Braised Chicken Wings *(page 6)*.
Pictured on the back cover *(top to bottom):* Pan-Cooked Bok Choy Salmon *(page 26),* Icy Mandarin Dessert *(page 78)* and Savory Pork Stir-Fry *(page 74).*

ISBN-13: 978-1-4127-5713-3
ISBN-10: 1-4127-5713-4

Manufactured in China.

8 7 6 5 4 3 2 1

TABLE OF CONTENTS

SMALL BITES

Soy-Braised Chicken Wings
MAKES 2 DOZEN WINGS

¼ **cup dry sherry**

¼ **cup soy sauce**

2 **tablespoons sugar**

2 **tablespoons cornstarch**

2 **tablespoons minced garlic, divided**

2 **teaspoons red pepper flakes**

12 **chicken wings (about 2½ pounds), tips removed and cut into halves**

2 **tablespoons vegetable oil**

3 **green onions, cut into 1-inch pieces**

¼ **cup chicken broth**

1 **teaspoon sesame oil**

1 **tablespoon sesame seeds, toasted***

*To toast sesame seeds, spread seeds in small skillet. Shake skillet over medium-low heat until seeds begin to pop and turn golden, about 3 minutes.

1. For marinade, combine sherry, soy sauce, sugar, cornstarch, 1 tablespoon garlic and red pepper flakes in large bowl; mix well. Reserve ¼ cup marinade. Stir in chicken wings; cover and marinate in refrigerator overnight, turning once or twice.

2. Drain wings; discard marinade. Heat wok over high heat 1 minute. Add 1 tablespoon vegetable oil; heat 30 seconds. Add half of wings; cook 5 to 10 minutes or until wings are brown on all sides, turning occasionally. Remove with slotted spoon to bowl. Repeat with remaining oil and wings. Reduce heat to medium.

3. Add remaining 1 tablespoon garlic and green onions to wok; cook and stir 30 seconds. Add wings and broth. Cover and cook 5 to 10 minutes or until wings are cooked through, stirring occasionally.

4. Add sesame oil to reserved marinade; mix well. Add to wok; cook and stir 2 minutes or until wings are glazed with marinade. Transfer to serving platter; sprinkle with sesame seeds. Serve immediately.

Hors D'oeuvre Triangles

MAKES 40 TRIANGLES

Sweet and Sour Sauce (recipe follows)

½ **cup Chinese-style thin egg noodles, broken into 1-inch pieces**

2 **tablespoons butter**

¼ **pound ground pork**

6 **fresh medium mushrooms, finely chopped**

6 **green onions, finely chopped**

8 **ounces cooked shrimp, peeled, deveined and finely chopped**

1 **hard-cooked egg, finely chopped**

1 **tablespoon plus 1½ teaspoons dry sherry**

½ **teaspoon salt**

⅛ **teaspoon black pepper**

40 **wonton wrappers**

1 **egg, lightly beaten**

Vegetable oil for frying

1. Prepare Sweet and Sour Sauce; set aside.

2. Cook noodles according to package directions; drain well.

3. Heat butter in wok or large skillet over medium-high heat. Add pork; brown about 5 minutes, stirring to break up meat. Add mushrooms and green onions; stir-fry 2 minutes.

4. Remove wok from heat. Add noodles, shrimp, egg, sherry, salt and pepper; mix well. Spoon 1 tablespoon pork mixture across center of each wonton wrapper. Brush edges lightly with beaten egg. Fold in half, making points meet to form triangle; pinch edges slightly to seal.

5. Heat oil in wok or large skillet to 375°F. Add 4 to 6 rolls at a time; cook until golden and crisp, 3 to 5 minutes. Drain on paper towels. Serve with Sweet and Sour Sauce.

Sweet and Sour Sauce

1 **cup water**

½ **cup sugar**

½ **cup white vinegar**

¼ **cup tomato paste**

4 **teaspoons cornstarch**

Combine all ingredients in small saucepan. Bring to a boil over medium heat. Boil 1 minute, stirring constantly.

Lobster Pot Stickers

MAKES ABOUT 26 POT STICKERS

Chinese Dipping Sauce (recipe follows)

4 dried black Chinese mushrooms

8 ounces lobster flavored surimi, finely chopped

2 cups chopped Napa cabbage or green cabbage

¼ cup chopped green onions

1 tablespoon minced fresh ginger

2 teaspoons sesame oil

2 teaspoons soy sauce

26 wonton wrappers

2 tablespoons vegetable oil, divided

1 cup chicken broth, divided

1. Prepare Chinese Dipping Sauce; set aside.

2. Place mushrooms in medium bowl; cover with warm water. Soak 20 to 40 minutes or until soft. Drain; discard water. Cut off and discard stems. Chop caps; return to bowl.

3. Place lobster, cabbage, green onions, ginger, sesame oil and soy sauce in large bowl; toss lightly.

4. To make pot stickers, cut ½-inch triangle off all corners of wonton wrappers to make rounded shapes. Working in batches, place about 2 teaspoons lobster mixture in center of each wrapper. Lightly moisten edges with water; fold in half. Pinch edges together to seal. Cover finished pot stickers with plastic wrap.

5. Heat 1 tablespoon vegetable oil in large nonstick skillet over medium heat. Place half of pot stickers in skillet.

Cook 5 to 6 minutes or until bottoms are golden brown, turning once.

6. Add ½ cup broth to skillet; reduce heat to low. Cover and simmer 10 minutes or until all liquid is absorbed (15 minutes if pot stickers were frozen). Repeat with remaining vegetable oil, pot stickers and broth.

7. Serve with Chinese Dipping Sauce.

Chinese Dipping Sauce

¼ cup soy sauce

1 tablespoon rice vinegar

1 teaspoon dark sesame oil

Combine all ingredients in small bowl. Makes about ¼ cup.

Tip: Pot stickers may be cooked immediately or covered securely and stored in refrigerator up to 4 hours or frozen up to 3 months. To freeze, place pot stickers on cookie sheet or shallow pan; freeze 30 minutes to firm slightly. Remove from freezer; place in food storage freezer bag. (Frozen pot stickers do not need to be thawed before cooking.)

春 **SMALL BITES**

Mustard-Glazed Shrimp

MAKES 6 TO 8 APPETIZER SERVINGS

MAZOLA PURE® Cooking Spray

1 tablespoon dry mustard

2 tablespoons hot water

¼ cup KARO® Light or Dark Corn Syrup

¼ cup prepared duck or plum sauce

2 tablespoons rice wine or sake

1 tablespoon soy sauce

1 tablespoon dark Oriental sesame oil

1 pound large shrimp, shelled and deveined, or sea scallops

¾ pound sliced bacon, cut crosswise in half

Bamboo skewers, soaked in cold water 20 minutes

1. Line broiler pan rack with foil; spray with cooking spray.

2. In small bowl stir mustard and water until smooth. Stir in corn syrup, duck sauce, rice wine, soy sauce and sesame oil.

3. In large bowl toss shrimp with about ¼ cup of the mustard glaze. Wrap half slice bacon around each shrimp and thread about 1 inch apart onto skewers.

4. Broil 6 inches from heat, 8 to 10 minutes or until shrimp are tender, turning and brushing occasionally with remaining mustard glaze.

Oriental Beef Skewers

MAKES 40 APPETIZERS

¼ cup **KARO® Light or Dark Corn Syrup**

1 tablespoon **ARGO® or KINGSFORD'S® Corn Starch**

½ cup **soy sauce**

3 tablespoons **MAZOLA® Corn Oil**

2 tablespoons **sesame seeds**

2 cloves **garlic, minced**

1 teaspoon **pepper**

½ teaspoon **grated fresh ginger**

2 pounds **beef top round steak (1-inch thick), cut into 1-inch pieces**

½ cup **chopped green onions**

1. In 13×9×2-inch baking dish stir corn syrup, corn starch, soy sauce, corn oil, sesame seeds, garlic, pepper and ginger until smooth. Add beef and green onions; toss to coat.

2. Cover; refrigerate at least 4 hours or overnight.

3. Drain beef, reserving marinade. Place beef cubes on broiler rack.

4. Broil 6 inches from source of heat, turning occasionally and brushing with reserved marinade, 6 to 8 minutes or until meat is browned on all sides.

5. Serve with cocktail picks.

Note:

Round steak is a less tender cut of meat. To keep the cubes moist and tender, broil just to medium-rare. Or, substitute beef top sirloin or tenderloin for delicious juicy morsels.

春

Baked Egg Rolls

MAKES 12 EGG ROLLS

Sesame Dipping Sauce (recipe follows)

1 ounce dried shiitake mushrooms

1 large carrot, shredded

1 can (8 ounces) sliced water chestnuts, drained and minced

3 green onions, minced

3 tablespoons chopped fresh cilantro

Nonstick cooking spray

12 ounces ground chicken

2 tablespoons minced fresh ginger

6 cloves garlic, minced

2 tablespoons soy sauce

2 teaspoons water

1 teaspoon cornstarch

12 egg roll wrappers

1 tablespoon vegetable oil

1 teaspoon sesame seeds

1. Prepare Sesame Dipping Sauce; set aside.

2. Place mushrooms in small bowl. Cover with warm water; let stand 30 minutes or until tender. Rinse well; drain, squeezing out excess water. Cut off and discard stems; finely chop caps. Combine mushrooms, carrot, water chestnuts, green onions and cilantro in large bowl.

3. Spray medium nonstick skillet with cooking spray; heat over medium-high heat. Brown chicken 2 minutes, stirring to break up meat. Add ginger and garlic; cook and stir 2 minutes more,

until chicken is cooked through. Add to mushroom mixture. Sprinkle with soy sauce; mix thoroughly.

4. Preheat oven to 425°F. Spray baking sheet with cooking spray; set aside. Blend water into cornstarch in small bowl. Lay 1 wrapper on work surface. Spoon about ⅓ cup filling across center of wrapper to within about ½ inch of sides. Fold bottom of wrapper over filling. Fold in sides. Brush ½-inch strip across top edge with cornstarch mixture; roll up and seal. Place seam side down on baking sheet. Repeat with remaining wrappers.

5. Brush egg rolls with oil. Sprinkle with sesame seeds. Bake 18 minutes or until golden and crisp. Serve with Sesame Dipping Sauce.

Sesame Dipping Sauce

½ cup rice vinegar

4 teaspoons soy sauce

2 teaspoons minced fresh ginger

1 teaspoon dark sesame oil

Combine all ingredients in small bowl; blend well. Makes about ½ cup.

Fried Tofu with Sesame Dipping Sauce

MAKES 8 PIECES

3 tablespoons soy sauce or tamari

2 tablespoons unseasoned rice wine vinegar

2 teaspoons sugar

1 teaspoon sesame seeds, toasted*

1 teaspoon dark sesame oil

⅛ teaspoon red pepper flakes

1 package (about 14 ounces) extra-firm tofu

2 tablespoons all-purpose flour

1 egg

¾ cup panko bread crumbs**

4 tablespoons vegetable oil

*To toast sesame seeds, spread seeds in small skillet. Shake skillet over medium-low heat until seeds begin to pop and turn golden, about 3 minutes.

**Panko bread crumbs are used in Japanese cooking to provide a crisp exterior to fried foods. They are coarser than ordinary bread crumbs. You'll find panko in the Asian aisle of large supermarkets.

1. For dipping sauce, combine soy sauce, vinegar, sugar, sesame seeds, sesame oil and red pepper flakes in small bowl. Set aside.

2. Drain tofu and press between paper towels to remove excess water. Cut crosswise into 4 slices; cut each slice diagonally into triangles. Place flour in shallow dish. Beat egg in shallow bowl. Place panko in another shallow bowl.

3. Dip each piece of tofu in flour to coat all sides; dip in egg, turning to coat. Drain and roll in panko to coat lightly.

4. Heat 2 tablespoons vegetable oil in large nonstick skillet over high heat. Reduce heat to medium; add 4 pieces of tofu in single layer. Cook 1 to 2 minutes per side or until golden brown. Repeat with remaining tofu. Serve with dipping sauce.

QUICK-FIX
RECIPES

道

Hoisin-Orange Chicken Wraps
MAKES 4 SERVINGS

¼ cup hoisin sauce

½ teaspoon grated orange peel

¼ cup orange juice

8 whole Boston lettuce leaves

2 cups shredded coleslaw mix

2 cups diced cooked chicken
   (about 8 ounces)

Black pepper

1. Combine hoisin sauce, orange peel and juice in small bowl.

2. Arrange lettuce leaves on large serving platter. Place ¼ cup coleslaw mix, ¼ cup chicken and 1 tablespoon hoisin mixture on each leaf. Sprinkle with pepper.

3. Fold lettuce over filling to create wraps.

Tip: Oranges store well and can be purchased in large quantities. One medium orange yields ⅓ to ½ cup juice. The rind of 1 medium orange yields 1 to 2 tablespoons grated peel.

Pineapple Basil Chicken Supreme

MAKES 4 SERVINGS

1 can (8 ounces) pineapple chunks in unsweetened juice

2 teaspoons cornstarch

2 tablespoons peanut oil

1 pound boneless skinless chicken breasts, cut into ¾-inch pieces

2 to 4 serrano peppers,* cut into thin strips (optional)

2 cloves garlic, minced

2 green onions, cut into 1-inch pieces

¾ cup roasted unsalted cashews

¼ cup chopped fresh basil (do not use dried)

1 tablespoon fish sauce**

1 tablespoon soy sauce

Hot cooked rice

*Serrano peppers can sting and irritate the skin, so wear rubber gloves when handling peppers and do not touch your eyes.

**Fish sauce is available at most large supermarkets and Asian markets.

1. Drain pineapple, reserving juice. Combine juice and cornstarch in small bowl; set aside.

2. Heat wok or large skillet over high heat 1 minute. Drizzle oil into wok; heat 30 seconds. Add chicken, serrano peppers, if desired, and garlic; stir-fry 3 minutes or until chicken is cooked through. Add green onions; stir-fry 1 minute.

3. Stir cornstarch mixture; add to wok. Cook and stir 1 minute or until thickened. Add pineapple, cashews, basil, fish sauce and soy sauce; cook and stir 1 minute or until heated through. Serve over rice.

Bistro in a Pot

MAKES 4 TO 6 SERVINGS

2 tablespoons extra virgin olive oil

½ to 1 pound boneless skinless chicken, cut into bite-size pieces

½ cup minced shallots

2 large cloves garlic, sliced

2 cups chopped leeks, white and light green parts, washed and drained

1½ cups baby carrots, cut into quarters lengthwise

1 cup thinly sliced new potatoes

2 tablespoons dried tarragon

3 to 4 teaspoons dried lemon peel

½ cup water

1 cup shredded JARLSBERG LITE™ cheese

1 cup frozen peas, thawed (optional)

Minced fresh parsley for garnish

In wok or large skillet with cover, heat olive oil over high heat until nearly smoking. Stir-fry chicken, shallots and garlic. Remove to bowl. Add leeks to wok and stir-fry 3 minutes. Add to chicken mixture. Add carrots, potatoes, tarragon and lemon peel to wok; stir-fry 5 minutes. Return chicken mixture to wok. Add ½ cup water; stir quickly. Cover tightly and steam 5 minutes. (Add more water if necessary.)

Remove from heat; add cheese and peas, if desired. Stir and serve. Garnish with parsley.

Exotic Pork & Vegetables
MAKES 4 SERVINGS

¼ **cup water**

2 **teaspoons cornstarch**

4 **tablespoons peanut oil, divided**

6 **whole dried hot red chili peppers**

4 **cloves garlic, sliced**

1 **pork tenderloin (about ¾ pound), thinly sliced**

1 **large carrot, cut into ¼-inch-thick slices***

2 **ounces fresh oyster, shiitake or button mushrooms,** ** **halved**

1 **baby eggplant, thinly sliced**

5 **ounces fresh snow peas, ends trimmed**

3 **tablespoons packed brown sugar**

2 **tablespoons fish sauce**

1 **tablespoon dark sesame oil**

Hot cooked rice

*To make scalloped edges on carrot, use citrus stripper or grapefruit spoon to cut groove into carrot, cutting lengthwise from stem end to tip. Continue to cut grooves around carrot about ¼ inch apart. Then cut carrot crosswise into ¼-inch-thick slices.

**Or, substitute ½ ounce dried shiitake mushrooms, soaked according to package directions.

1. Stir water into cornstarch in small bowl until well blended; set aside.

2. Heat wok or large skillet 1 minute over high heat. Drizzle 2 tablespoons peanut oil into wok; heat 30 seconds. Add peppers and garlic; stir-fry about 1 minute. Add pork; stir-fry 3 to 4 minutes or until barely pink in center. Remove pork mixture to bowl.

3. Add remaining 2 tablespoons peanut oil to wok. Add carrot, mushrooms and eggplant; stir-fry 2 minutes. Add snow peas and pork mixture; stir-fry 1 minute.

4. Stir cornstarch mixture; add to wok. Cook 1 minute or until sauce thickens. Stir in brown sugar, fish sauce and sesame oil; cook and stir until heated through. Serve with rice.

Pan-Cooked Bok Choy Salmon

MAKES 2 SERVINGS

1 pound bok choy or napa cabbage, chopped

1 cup broccoli slaw mix

2 tablespoons olive oil, divided

2 salmon fillets (4 to 6 ounces each)

¼ teaspoon salt

½ teaspoon black pepper

1 teaspoon sesame seeds

1. Combine bok choy and broccoli slaw mix in colander; rinse and drain well.

2. Heat 1 tablespoon oil in large nonstick skillet over medium heat. Sprinkle salmon with salt and pepper. Add salmon to skillet; cook about 3 minutes per side. Remove salmon from skillet.

3. Add remaining 1 tablespoon oil and sesame seeds to skillet; stir to toast sesame seeds. Add bok choy mixture; cook and stir 3 to 4 minutes.

4. Return salmon to skillet. Reduce heat to low; cover and cook about 4 minutes or until salmon begins to flake when tested with fork.

Tip: Bok choy stalks have a crisp texture and a mild cabbage-like flavor. The leaves take on a mild flavor similar to Swiss chard. Available all year, bok choy is also sometimes referred to as Chinese chard, pak chois, white mustard cabbage or Chinese mustard. It is usually sold by the pound.

Five-Spice Beef Stir-Fry

MAKES 4 SERVINGS

1 boneless beef top sirloin steak (about 1 pound)

2 tablespoons soy sauce

2 tablespoons plus 1½ teaspoons cornstarch, divided

3 tablespoons walnut or vegetable oil, divided

4 medium carrots, cut into matchstick-size pieces (about 2 cups)

3 cups hot cooked rice

1 red bell pepper, cut into 1-inch pieces

1 yellow bell pepper, cut into 1-inch pieces

1 cup chopped onion

¼ to ½ teaspoon red pepper flakes

1½ cups water

1 tablespoon plus 1½ teaspoons packed dark brown sugar

2 teaspoons beef bouillon granules

1 teaspoon Chinese five-spice powder*

½ cup honey-roasted peanuts

Chinese five-spice powder is a blend of cinnamon, cloves, fennel seed, anise and Szechuan peppercorns. It is available in most supermarkets and at Asian grocery stores.

1. Cut steak in half lengthwise, then cut crosswise into thin strips. Place beef in shallow glass baking dish. Stir soy sauce into 2 tablespoons cornstarch in small bowl until well blended. Pour soy sauce mixture over beef; toss to coat.

2. Meanwhile, heat 1 tablespoon oil in large nonstick skillet or wok 1 minute over high heat. Add carrots; stir-fry 3 to 4 minutes or until edges begin to brown. Combine carrots and rice in large serving bowl; toss well. Cover and keep warm.

3. Reduce heat to medium-high. Add 1 tablespoon oil, bell peppers, onion and red pepper flakes; stir-fry 4 minutes or until onion is translucent. Remove pepper mixture to large bowl; set aside.

4. Add remaining 1 tablespoon oil to skillet. Add half of beef; stir-fry 2 minutes or until beef is barely pink in center. Add beef to pepper mixture. Repeat with remaining beef.

5. Combine water, brown sugar, bouillon granules, five-spice powder and remaining 1½ teaspoons cornstarch in small bowl; stir until smooth. Add bouillon mixture and beef mixture to skillet; bring to a boil. Cook and stir 2 to 3 minutes or until sauce is slightly thickened.

6. Spoon beef mixture over rice; sprinkle with peanuts.

Sesame Chicken

MAKES 4 SERVINGS

1 pound boneless skinless chicken breasts or thighs

⅔ cup teriyaki sauce, divided

2 teaspoons cornstarch

1 tablespoon peanut or vegetable oil

2 cloves garlic, minced

2 green onions, cut into ½-inch slices

1 tablespoon sesame seeds, toasted*

1 teaspoon dark sesame oil

*To toast sesame seeds, spread seeds in small skillet. Shake skillet over medium-low heat 3 minutes or until seeds begin to pop and turn golden.

1. Cut chicken into 1-inch pieces; toss with ⅓ cup teriyaki sauce in medium bowl. Marinate 30 minutes in refrigerator.

2. Drain chicken; discard marinade. Blend remaining ⅓ cup teriyaki sauce into cornstarch in small bowl until smooth.

3. Heat peanut oil in wok or large skillet over medium-high heat. Add chicken and garlic; stir-fry 3 minutes or until chicken is cooked through. Stir cornstarch mixture; add to wok. Cook and stir 1 minute or until sauce boils and thickens.

4. Stir in green onions, sesame seeds and sesame oil. Serve immediately.

Sweet and Sour Pork

MAKES 4 SERVINGS

1 tablespoon soy sauce

2 cloves garlic, minced

1 pound pork loin or tenderloin*

1 can (8 ounces) pineapple chunks in juice, undrained

2 tablespoons peanut or vegetable oil, divided

2 medium carrots, diagonally cut into thin slices

1 large green bell pepper, cut into 1-inch pieces

⅓ cup stir-fry sauce

1 tablespoon white wine vinegar or white vinegar

Hot cooked rice

Or, substitute 1 pound boneless skinless chicken breasts or thighs.

1. Combine soy sauce and garlic in medium bowl. Cut pork into 1-inch pieces; toss with soy sauce mixture.

2. Drain pineapple, reserving 2 tablespoons juice.

3. Heat wok or large skillet over medium-high heat. Add 1 tablespoon oil; heat 30 seconds. Add pork mixture; stir-fry 4 to 5 minutes or until pork is barely pink in center. Remove pork from wok; set aside.

4. Heat remaining 1 tablespoon oil in wok. Add carrots and bell pepper; stir-fry 4 to 5 minutes or until vegetables are crisp-tender. Add pineapple; stir-fry until heated through.

5. Add stir-fry sauce, reserved pineapple juice and vinegar to wok; stir-fry 30 seconds or until sauce comes to a boil.

6. Return pork along with any accumulated juices to wok; cook and stir until heated through. Serve over rice.

Lemon Sesame Scallops

MAKES 4 SERVINGS

1 tablespoon sesame seeds

8 ounces uncooked whole wheat spaghetti

3 tablespoons sesame oil, divided

¼ cup chicken broth or clam juice

½ teaspoon grated lemon peel

3 tablespoons lemon juice

2 tablespoons oyster sauce

1 tablespoon cornstarch

1 tablespoon soy sauce

1 tablespoon vegetable oil

2 carrots, cut into julienne strips

1 yellow bell pepper, cut into thin strips

4 slices peeled fresh ginger

1 clove garlic, minced

1 pound sea scallops

6 ounces fresh snow peas, trimmed or 1 package (6 ounces) frozen snow peas, thawed

2 green onions, thinly sliced

1. Heat small skillet over medium-low heat. Add sesame seeds; cook and stir about 3 minutes or until golden; set aside.

2. Cook spaghetti according to package directions; drain. Place in large bowl; toss with 2 tablespoons sesame oil. Cover to keep warm.

3. Blend broth, lemon peel, lemon juice, oyster sauce, cornstarch and soy sauce in small bowl until smooth; set aside.

4. Heat remaining 1 tablespoon sesame oil and vegetable oil in large skillet or wok over medium heat. Add carrots and bell pepper; stir-fry 4 to 5 minutes or until crisp-tender. Transfer to large bowl.

5. Add ginger and garlic to skillet; stir-fry 1 minute over medium-high heat. Add scallops; stir-fry 1 minute. Add snow peas and green onions; stir-fry 2 to 3 minutes or until scallops are opaque. Remove and discard ginger. Transfer scallop mixture to bowl with vegetable mixture, leaving any liquid in skillet.

6. Stir broth mixture; add to skillet. Cook and stir 5 minutes or until thickened. Return scallop mixture to skillet; cook 1 minute or until heated through. Serve immediately over warm spaghetti; sprinkle with sesame seeds.

Better-Than-Take-Out Fried Rice
MAKES 4 SERVINGS

3 tablespoons soy sauce

1 tablespoon rice vinegar

⅛ teaspoon red pepper flakes

1 medium red bell pepper

1 tablespoon peanut or vegetable oil

6 green onions, cut into 1-inch pieces

1 tablespoon grated fresh ginger

1½ teaspoons minced garlic

½ pound boneless pork loin or tenderloin, cut into 1-inch pieces

2 cups shredded coleslaw mix

1 package (8½ ounces) cooked brown rice

1. Combine soy sauce, vinegar and red pepper flakes in small bowl; mix well.

2. Cut bell pepper into decorative shapes using 1¼- to 1½-inch cookie cutters or cut into 1-inch pieces.

3. Heat oil in large nonstick skillet or wok over medium-high heat. Add bell pepper, green onions, ginger and garlic; stir-fry 1 minute. Add pork; stir-fry 2 to 3 minutes or until pork is barely pink in center.

4. Stir in coleslaw mix, rice and soy sauce mixture; cook and stir 1 minute or until heated through.

Easy Make-at-Home Chinese Chicken

MAKES 4 SERVINGS

3 tablespoons frozen orange juice concentrate, thawed

2 tablespoons water

2 tablespoons soy sauce

¾ teaspoon cornstarch

¼ teaspoon garlic powder

Nonstick cooking spray

2 carrots, cut into ¼-inch slices

12 ounces frozen broccoli and cauliflower florets, thawed

1 tablespoon vegetable oil

¾ pound boneless skinless chicken breasts, cut into bite-size pieces

1⅓ cups hot cooked rice

1. For sauce, stir together orange juice concentrate, water, soy sauce, cornstarch and garlic powder; set aside.

2. Spray nonstick wok or large skillet with cooking spray. Add carrots; stir-fry over high heat 1 minute. Add broccoli and cauliflower; stir-fry 2 to 3 minutes or until vegetables are crisp-tender. Remove vegetables from wok; set aside.

3. Add oil to wok; heat over medium-high heat. Stir-fry chicken 2 to 3 minutes or until cooked through. Push chicken up side of wok. Stir sauce; add to wok. Bring to a boil. Return vegetables to wok; cook and stir until heated through. Serve over rice.

Tip: To cut carrots decoratively, use a citrus stripper or grapefruit spoon to cut 4 or 5 grooves into whole carrots, cutting lengthwise from stem end to tip. Then cut carrots crosswise into slices.

Savoy Shrimp

MAKES 4 SERVINGS

1 pound large raw shrimp (about 20), peeled and deveined (with tails on)

½ teaspoon Chinese five-spice powder*

2 tablespoons dark sesame oil

4 cups sliced savoy or napa cabbage

1 cup snow peas, trimmed

1 tablespoon diced candied ginger (optional)

1 tablespoon soy sauce

1 teaspoon red pepper flakes

½ teaspoon ground ginger

Juice of 1 lime

¼ cup chopped fresh cilantro (optional)

*Chinese five-spice powder is a blend of cinnamon, cloves, fennel seed, anise and Szechuan peppercorns. It is available in most supermarkets and at Asian grocery stores.

1. Rinse shrimp; drain well. Toss with Chinese five-spice powder; set aside.

2. Heat oil in large nonstick skillet over medium heat. Add cabbage, snow peas, candied ginger, if desired, soy sauce, red pepper flakes and ground ginger. Cook and stir until cabbage is tender.

3. Add shrimp and lime juice; stir. Cover skillet; reduce heat to low. Cook 3 minutes or until shrimp are pink and opaque. Garnish with cilantro.

Szechuan Pork Stir-Fry over Spinach

MAKES 2 SERVINGS

2 teaspoons dark sesame oil, divided

¾ cup matchstick-size carrot strips

½ pound pork tenderloin, cut into thin strips

3 cloves garlic, minced

2 teaspoons minced fresh ginger

¼ teaspoon red pepper flakes

1 tablespoon soy sauce

1 tablespoon mirin* or dry sherry

2 teaspoons cornstarch

8 ounces baby spinach

2 teaspoons sesame seeds, toasted**

*Mirin, a sweet wine made from rice, is an essential flavoring in Japanese cuisine. It is available in Asian markets and the Asian or gourmet section of some supermarkets.

**To toast sesame seeds, spread in small skillet. Shake skillet over medium-low heat about 3 minutes or until seeds begin to pop and turn golden.

1. Heat 1 teaspoon oil in large nonstick skillet over medium-high heat. Add carrot strips. Cook 3 minutes, stirring occasionally. Add pork, garlic, ginger and red pepper flakes. Stir-fry 3 minutes or until pork is barely pink in center.

2. Stir soy sauce, mirin and cornstarch in small bowl until well blended; add to pork mixture. Stir-fry about 1 minute or until sauce thickens.

3. Heat remaining 1 teaspoon oil in medium saucepan over medium-high heat. Add spinach. Cover and cook until spinach is barely wilted, about 1 minute. Transfer spinach to 2 serving plates. Spoon pork mixture over spinach. Sprinkle with sesame seeds.

Chinese Skillet Chicken and Rice

MAKES 4 SERVINGS

½ teaspoon red pepper flakes

½ teaspoon Chinese five-spice powder*

¼ teaspoon white pepper

4 boneless skinless chicken breasts

2 teaspoons vegetable oil

1 large onion, chopped

2 cloves garlic, minced

1 cup uncooked rice

1¼ cups chicken broth

½ cup water

1 tablespoon soy sauce

2 red bell peppers, sliced

1 cup fresh bean sprouts

1 cup sliced fresh mushrooms

1 cup frozen peas, thawed

¾ cup canned water chestnuts, drained

1 teaspoon minced fresh ginger

Chinese five-spice powder is a blend of cinnamon, cloves, fennel seed, anise and Szechuan peppercorns. It is available in most supermarkets and at Asian grocery stores.

1. Combine red pepper flakes, five-spice powder and white pepper in small bowl. Rub onto all surfaces of chicken. Heat oil in large nonstick skillet over medium heat. Add chicken; cook 5 minutes. Turn chicken; cook 5 minutes. Remove from skillet; set aside.

2. Cook onion and garlic in drippings 3 minutes, stirring occasionally. Add rice; stir to coat. Stir in broth, water and soy sauce. Bring to a boil over high heat; reduce heat to medium.

3. Arrange chicken and bell peppers over rice in skillet. Cover and simmer 15 minutes or until most of the liquid is absorbed and chicken is no longer pink in center. Remove from heat; stir bean sprouts, mushrooms, peas, water chestnuts and ginger into rice. Cover; let stand 10 minutes.

Ginger-Mint Stir-Fry Chicken

MAKES 4 TO 6 SERVINGS

6 to 8 dried shiitake mushrooms (½ ounce)

2 tablespoons packed brown sugar

2 tablespoons fish sauce

2 tablespoons rice vinegar

4 to 6 teaspoons vegetable oil, divided

1½ pounds boneless skinless chicken breasts or thighs, cut into ½-inch strips

1 or 2 jalapeño peppers,* seeded and chopped

2 tablespoons finely chopped fresh ginger

3 cloves garlic, minced

1 large carrot, cut into thin slices

1 can (5½ ounces) whole baby corn, drained

4 green onions, cut into 1-inch pieces

¼ cup slivered fresh mint leaves

Hot cooked rice

Jalapeño peppers can sting and irritate the skin, so wear rubber gloves when handling peppers and do not touch your eyes.

1. Place mushrooms in bowl; cover with hot water. Let stand 30 minutes or until caps are soft. Drain mushrooms; squeeze out excess water. Remove and discard stems. Slice caps into thin strips.

2. Combine brown sugar, fish sauce and vinegar in small bowl; stir until sugar is dissolved.

3. Heat wok or large skillet over high heat. Heat 2 teaspoons oil in wok. Add one third of chicken; stir-fry 3 minutes or until chicken is cooked through. Transfer to bowl. Repeat twice with remaining chicken, adding 1 teaspoon oil with each batch to prevent sticking, if necessary.

4. Add remaining 2 teaspoons oil to wok. Add jalapeño peppers, ginger and garlic; stir-fry 1 to 2 minutes or until fragrant but not browned.

5. Add fish sauce mixture to wok; boil until reduced by half. Return chicken to wok. Add mushrooms, carrot, baby corn and green onions; stir-fry 2 to 3 minutes or until heated through. Stir in mint. Serve with rice.

LIGHT & EASY

夏

Tofu and Snow Pea Noodle Bowl

MAKES 4 SERVINGS

5 cups water

6 tablespoons chicken or vegetarian broth powder*

4 ounces uncooked vermicelli, broken in thirds

½ pound firm tofu, rinsed, patted dry and cut in ¼-inch cubes

3 ounces snow peas

1 cup matchstick-size carrot strips**

½ teaspoon chili garlic sauce

½ cup chopped green onions

¼ cup chopped fresh cilantro (optional)

2 tablespoons lime juice

1 tablespoon grated fresh ginger

2 teaspoons soy sauce

Vegetarian broth powder can be found in natural food stores and some supermarkets.

**Matchstick-size carrot strips are sometimes called shredded carrots and may be sold with other prepared vegetables in the supermarket produce section.*

1. Bring water to a boil in large saucepan over high heat. Stir in broth powder and vermicelli. Return to a boil. Reduce heat to medium-high and simmer 6 minutes. Stir in tofu, snow peas, carrots and chili garlic sauce; simmer 2 minutes.

2. Remove from heat; stir in green onions, cilantro, if desired, lime juice, ginger and soy sauce. Serve immediately.

Tip: Substitute 5 cups chicken or vegetable broth for the water and broth powder.

夏 **LIGHT & EASY**

Sizzling Rice Cakes with Mushrooms and Bell Peppers

MAKES 4 TO 6 SERVINGS

¾ cup short grain rice*

1¾ cups water, divided

1 can (about 14 ounces) chicken broth

1 tablespoon soy sauce

2 teaspoons sugar

2 teaspoons red wine vinegar

2 tablespoons cornstarch

3 tablespoons peanut oil, divided

1½ teaspoons finely chopped fresh ginger

2 cloves garlic, thinly sliced

1 red bell pepper, cut into short strips

1 green bell pepper, cut into short strips

8 ounces button mushrooms, quartered

4 ounces fresh shiitake or other exotic mushrooms, sliced

1 teaspoon sesame oil

Vegetable oil for frying

Short grain rice is preferred for this recipe because of it's high starch content and sticky texture when cooked. It also may be referred to as pearl or glutinous rice. Look for it in most large supermarkets.

1. Rinse rice under cold running water to remove excess starch. Combine rice and 1½ cups water in medium saucepan.

2. Bring to a boil over medium-high heat. Reduce heat to low; cover and simmer 15 to 20 minutes until liquid is absorbed. Let cool.

3. Combine broth, soy sauce, sugar and vinegar in medium bowl. Combine cornstarch and remaining ¼ cup water in small cup; mix well. Set aside.

4. Heat 1 tablespoon peanut oil in wok over medium-high heat. Add ginger and garlic; stir-fry 10 seconds. Add pepper strips; stir-fry 2 to 3 minutes or until crisp-tender. Remove and set aside.

5. Add remaining 2 tablespoons peanut oil to wok. Add mushrooms; stir-fry 2 to 3 minutes or until softened. Remove and set aside.

6. Add broth mixture to wok and bring to a boil. Stir cornstarch mixture; add to wok. Cook and stir until sauce boils and thickens slightly. Stir in sesame oil; return vegetables to wok. Remove from heat; cover to keep warm.

7. Shape rice into 12 (2-inch) cakes. (Wet hands to make handling rice easier.)

8. Heat 2 to 3 inches vegetable oil in large skillet over medium-high heat until oil registers 375°F on deep-fry thermometer. Add 4 rice cakes; cook 2 to 3 minutes or until puffed and golden, turning occasionally. Remove with slotted spatula to paper towels. Repeat with remaining rice cakes, reheating oil between batches.

9. Place rice cakes in serving bowl. Stir vegetable mixture; pour over rice cakes.

Oriental Salad Supreme
MAKES 4 SERVINGS

¼ **cup peanut or vegetable oil**

¼ **cup rice vinegar**

2 **tablespoons brown sugar**

1 **medium unpeeled cucumber,
    halved lengthwise and sliced**

6 **cups torn romaine or leaf lettuce**

1 **cup chow mein noodles**

¼ **cup peanut halves or coarsely
    chopped cashews**

1. Combine oil, vinegar and brown sugar in small bowl; whisk until sugar dissolves. Toss with cucumber. Marinate, covered, in refrigerator up to 4 hours.

2. To serve, toss cucumber and marinade with lettuce, noodles and peanuts in large serving bowl.

Note:

Heighten the flavor of the salad by adding ¼ to ½ teaspoon red pepper flakes to the oil and vinegar marinade. For extra color, add thinly sliced radishes or carrots.

夏 **LIGHT &
EASY**

Chinese Sweet and Sour Vegetables

MAKES 4 SERVINGS

3 cups broccoli florets

2 medium carrots, diagonally sliced

1 large red bell pepper, cut into short, thin strips

¼ cup water

2 teaspoons cornstarch

1 teaspoon sugar

⅓ cup unsweetened pineapple juice

1 tablespoon rice vinegar

1 tablespoon soy sauce

½ teaspoon dark sesame oil

¼ cup chopped fresh cilantro (optional)

1. Combine broccoli, carrots and bell pepper in large skillet with tight-fitting lid. Add water; bring to a boil over high heat. Reduce heat to medium. Cover and steam 4 minutes or until vegetables are crisp-tender. Transfer vegetables to colander; drain.

2. Meanwhile, combine cornstarch and sugar in small bowl. Blend in pineapple juice, vinegar and soy sauce until smooth.

3. Stir cornstarch mixture; add to skillet. Cook and stir 2 minutes or until sauce boils and thickens. Return vegetables to skillet; toss with sauce. Stir in sesame oil. Garnish with cilantro.

Rice Noodles with Broccoli and Tofu

MAKES 4 TO 6 SERVINGS

1 package (14 ounces) firm or extra-firm tofu

1 package (8 to 10 ounces) wide rice noodles

2 tablespoons peanut oil

3 medium shallots, sliced

6 cloves garlic, minced

1 jalapeño pepper,* minced

2 teaspoons minced fresh ginger

3 cups broccoli florets

3 tablespoons regular soy sauce

1 tablespoon sweet soy sauce (or substitute regular)

1 to 2 tablespoons fish sauce

Fresh basil leaves (optional)

*Jalapeño peppers can sting and irritate the skin, so wear rubber gloves when handling peppers and do not touch your eyes.

1. Cut tofu crosswise in half. Place tofu on cutting board between layers of paper towels; put another cutting board on top to press moisture out of tofu. Soak rice noodles in large bowl filled with boiling water; let stand 30 minutes or until soft.

2. Cut tofu into bite-size squares. Heat oil in large skillet or wok over medium-high heat. Add tofu to skillet; stir-fry about 5 minutes or until tofu is lightly browned on all sides. Remove from skillet.

3. Add shallots, garlic, jalapeño pepper and ginger to skillet; stir-fry 2 to 3 minutes. Add broccoli; stir-fry 1 minute. Cover and cook 3 minutes or until broccoli is crisp-tender.

4. Drain noodles; stir into skillet. Return tofu to skillet; add soy sauces and fish sauce. Stir-fry about 8 minutes or until noodles are coated and flavors are blended. Garnish with basil.

Spinach and Mushroom Stir-Fry

MAKES 4 SERVINGS

2 tablespoons peanut oil

2 cloves garlic, minced

1 teaspoon minced fresh ginger

¼ to ½ teaspoon red pepper flakes

1 red bell pepper, cut into 1-inch pieces

2 ounces shiitake or button mushrooms,* sliced

10 ounces spinach, stemmed and coarsely chopped

1 teaspoon fish sauce

*Or, substitute ½ ounce dried shiitake mushrooms, soaked according to package directions.

1. Heat wok over high heat 1 minute. Drizzle oil into wok; heat 30 seconds. Add garlic, ginger and red pepper flakes; stir-fry 30 seconds.

2. Add bell pepper and mushrooms; stir-fry 2 minutes. Add spinach and fish sauce; stir-fry 1 to 2 minutes or until spinach is wilted.

夏 **LIGHT &
EASY**

Stir-Fried Asparagus
MAKES 6 SERVINGS

½ **pound asparagus**

1 **tablespoon olive or canola oil**

1 **cup sliced celery**

½ **cup roasted red peppers,
drained and diced**

¼ **cup sliced almonds, toasted***

¼ **teaspoon black pepper**

*To toast almonds, place in small dry skillet.
Cook over medium heat, stirring constantly,
until almonds are lightly browned.*

1. Trim and discard ends from asparagus.
Slice stalks diagonally into 1-inch
pieces.

2. Heat oil in 12-inch nonstick skillet
over medium-high heat. Add celery;
stir-fry 2 minutes. Add asparagus and
red peppers; stir-fry 3 to 4 minutes or
until asparagus is crisp-tender.

3. Add almonds and black pepper; stir
until blended.

Note:

When shopping for asparagus, remember that the size of the
asparagus stalk has no relationship to tenderness. Whether thick or
thin, select asparagus with firm, straight stalks and closed, compact
tips. Open tips are a sign of over-maturity. Also, always choose the
greenest asparagus.

Mongolian Vegetables

MAKES 2 MAIN-DISH OR 4 SIDE-DISH SERVINGS

1 package (about 14 ounces) firm tofu, drained

4 tablespoons soy sauce, divided

1 tablespoon dark sesame oil

1 large head bok choy (about 1½ pounds)

2 teaspoons cornstarch

1 tablespoon peanut or vegetable oil

1 large red or yellow bell pepper, cut into short, thin strips

2 cloves garlic, minced

4 green onions, cut into ½-inch pieces

2 teaspoons sesame seeds, toasted*

*To toast sesame seeds, spread seeds in small skillet. Shake skillet over medium-low heat 3 minutes or until seeds begin to pop and turn golden.

1. Press tofu between paper towels to remove excess water; cut into ¾-inch squares or triangles. Place in shallow dish. Combine 2 tablespoons soy sauce and sesame oil in small bowl; drizzle over tofu. Let stand while preparing vegetables.

2. Cut stems from bok choy leaves; slice stems into ½-inch pieces. Cut leaves crosswise into ½-inch slices.

3. Blend remaining 2 tablespoons soy sauce into cornstarch in small bowl until smooth.

4. Heat peanut oil in wok or large skillet over medium-high heat. Add bok choy stems, bell pepper and garlic; stir-fry 5 minutes. Add bok choy leaves and green onions; stir-fry 2 minutes.

5. Stir soy sauce mixture and add to wok along with tofu mixture. Stir-fry 30 seconds or until sauce boils and thickens. Sprinkle with sesame seeds.

夏 **LIGHT &** EASY

Hot Chinese Potatoes

MAKES 6 SERVINGS

3 tablespoons vegetable oil, divided

4 medium COLORADO Potatoes, halved lengthwise, thinly sliced

1 cup *each* thin diagonal carrot and celery slices

½ cup green bell pepper strips

½ cup sliced mushrooms

1 clove garlic, minced

½ cup water

2 tablespoons soy sauce

1½ teaspoons cornstarch

1 large tomato, cut into thin wedges

⅓ cup sliced green onions

Heat 1½ tablespoons oil in wok or large skillet. Add potatoes; cook and stir over medium-high heat about 10 minutes until barely tender. Remove and keep warm. Add remaining oil to wok. Add carrot, celery, pepper, mushrooms and garlic; cook and stir 3 to 4 minutes until crisp-tender.

Combine water, soy sauce and cornstarch in small bowl. Return potatoes to wok with cornstarch mixture. Cook and stir about 2 minutes, just until sauce thickens and mixture is heated through. Spoon onto platter; garnish with tomato and onions.

Favorite recipe from **Colorado Potato Administrative Committee**

Stir-Fried Spinach with Garlic

MAKES 2 SERVINGS

2 teaspoons peanut or vegetable oil

1 clove garlic, minced

6 cups packed torn stemmed spinach (about 8 ounces)

2 teaspoons soy sauce

1 teaspoon rice vinegar

¼ teaspoon sugar

1 teaspoon sesame seeds, toasted*

*To toast sesame seeds, spread seeds in small skillet. Shake skillet over medium heat 2 minutes or until seeds begin to pop and turn golden.

1. Heat wok or large skillet over medium-high heat. Add oil; heat 30 seconds. Add garlic; stir-fry 1 minute.

2. Add spinach, soy sauce, vinegar and sugar; stir-fry 1 to 2 minutes or until spinach is wilted. Sprinkle with sesame seeds.

Note:

If choosing loose spinach, look for leaves with good color and a crisp texture. Avoid limp, wilted, bruised, spotted or discolored leaves. The leaves should have a fresh aroma, not a sour or musty odor. Avoid leaves with thick coarse stems as they are a sign of overgrown spinach which can be tough and bitter. Thick stems also mean more waste since they are removed and discarded. If purchasing spinach prepackaged, squeeze the bag to check if the contents are fresh and crisp.

CHINESE CLASSICS

Orange Chicken

MAKES 4 SERVINGS

1 can (about 14 ounces) chicken broth, plus water to measure 3 cups

¾ cup wild rice, rinsed

1 cup orange juice

2 tablespoons teriyaki sauce

1 teaspoon cornstarch

1 teaspoon honey

2 cloves garlic, minced

Nonstick cooking spray

¾ pound boneless skinless chicken thighs, cut into thin strips

¼ cup dried currants

8 ounces (2½ to 3 cups) fresh snow peas or 1 package (6 ounces) frozen snow peas, thawed

1 orange, peeled and separated into segments

3 teaspoons grated orange peel, divided

3 green onions, thinly sliced

⅓ cup chopped fresh cilantro

1. Combine broth mixture and rice in large saucepan; bring to a boil over high heat. Reduce heat to low; simmer, partially covered, 45 to 55 minutes or until rice is tender. Drain off excess liquid; keep warm.

2. Blend orange juice, teriyaki sauce, cornstarch, honey and garlic in small bowl until smooth.

3. Spray large nonstick skillet with cooking spray; heat over high heat. Add chicken; stir-fry 4 minutes or until chicken is cooked through.

4. Stir orange juice mixture; add currants. Pour into skillet; boil, uncovered, 3 minutes. Add snow peas, orange segments and 1½ teaspoons orange peel. Cook and stir 2 minutes or until heated through. Stir in green onions and cilantro.

5. Spoon over rice. Sprinkle with remaining 1½ teaspoons orange peel.

Three-Topped Rice

MAKES 4 SERVINGS

2½ cups uncooked short grain rice

2¾ cups water

1 teaspoon salt, divided

2 tablespoons sugar, divided

2 tablespoons sake or dry sherry, divided

1 tablespoon plus 1 teaspoon soy sauce, divided

1 piece fresh ginger (about 1 inch), grated

8 ounces ground chicken

4 eggs

1½ cups cooked peas

1 ounce pickled ginger slices (optional)

1. Rinse rice under cold running water to remove excess starch. Combine rice, water and ½ teaspoon salt in large saucepan. Bring to a boil over medium-high heat. Reduce heat to low; cover and simmer about 15 minutes or until liquid is absorbed. Remove pan from heat; let stand, covered, 15 minutes. Gently fluff rice.

2. Combine 1 tablespoon sugar, 1 tablespoon sake, 1 tablespoon soy sauce and fresh ginger in medium saucepan; bring to a boil over high heat. Add chicken; cook and stir 3 to 4 minutes or until chicken is cooked through.

3. Combine eggs, remaining 1 tablespoon sugar, 1 tablespoon sake and 1 teaspoon soy sauce in small bowl; beat lightly. Spray large skillet with nonstick cooking spray; heat over medium-low heat. Add egg mixture; scramble until eggs are set but still moist.

4. Divide rice among 4 serving bowls. Place equal amounts of chicken, eggs and peas over rice. Garnish with pickled ginger.

Beef Teriyaki Stir-Fry

MAKES 4 SERVINGS

1 cup uncooked rice

1 boneless beef top sirloin steak (about 1 pound)

½ cup teriyaki sauce, divided

2 tablespoons vegetable oil, divided

1 medium onion, halved and sliced

2 cups frozen green beans, rinsed and drained

1. Cook rice according to package directions. Keep warm.

2. Cut beef lengthwise in half, then crosswise into ⅛-inch slices. Combine beef and ¼ cup teriyaki sauce in medium bowl; set aside.

3. Heat 1½ teaspoons oil in wok or large skillet over medium-high heat. Add onion; stir-fry 3 to 4 minutes or until crisp-tender. Remove from wok to another medium bowl.

4. Heat 1½ teaspoons oil in wok. Stir-fry green beans 3 minutes or until crisp-tender and hot. Drain off excess liquid. Add to onion in bowl.

5. Heat remaining 1 tablespoon oil in wok. Drain beef, discarding marinade. Stir-fry half of beef 2 minutes or until barely pink in center. Add to vegetables. Repeat with remaining beef. Return beef mixture to wok. Stir in remaining ¼ cup teriyaki sauce; cook and stir 1 minute or until heated through. Serve with rice.

Sweet and Sour Shrimp Stir-Fry
MAKES 4 SERVINGS

1 tablespoon dark sesame oil

½ cup thinly sliced celery

¼ cup chopped red bell pepper

¼ cup chopped green onions

½ teaspoon ground ginger

1 teaspoon sugar

1 teaspoon lemon juice

1 teaspoon soy sauce

1 pound medium raw shrimp, peeled and deveined

1. Heat oil in large nonstick skillet over medium heat. Add celery, bell pepper, green onions and ginger. Cook and stir 5 to 7 minutes.

2. Add sugar, lemon juice and soy sauce; cook and stir 1 minute. Add shrimp; cook 3 minutes or until shrimp are pink and opaque.

Tip: To peel shrimp, remove the legs by gently pulling them off the shell. Loosen the shell with your fingers, then slide it off. To devein shrimp, cut a shallow slit along the back of the shrimp with a paring knife. Lift out the vein.

Note:

Frozen peeled and deveined shrimp can be used in this recipe. To thaw, place the frozen shrimp in a colander and run cold water over them, separating them to help them thaw. Drain well before adding to the hot oil.

Cashew Chicken
MAKES 4 SERVINGS

1 pound boneless skinless chicken breasts or thighs

2 teaspoons minced fresh ginger

1 tablespoon peanut or vegetable oil

1 medium red bell pepper, cut into short, thin strips

⅓ cup teriyaki sauce

⅓ cup roasted or dry roasted cashews

Hot cooked rice

Coarsely chopped fresh cilantro (optional)

1. Cut chicken into ½-inch slices; cut each slice into 1½-inch strips. Toss chicken with ginger in small bowl.

2. Heat oil in wok or large skillet over medium-high heat. Add chicken mixture; stir-fry 2 minutes. Add bell pepper; stir-fry 4 minutes or until chicken is cooked through.

3. Add teriyaki sauce; stir-fry 1 minute or until sauce is heated through. Stir in cashews. Serve over rice. Garnish with cilantro.

Note:

Fresh ginger is completely different from dry ginger powder in both appearance and flavor. Resembling a gnarled, tan-colored root, fresh ginger adds its own distinctive pungency and aroma to foods, and is used extensively in the dishes of the Far East. Buy it in small quantities and store it, unpeeled, tightly wrapped in the refrigerator for up to 2 weeks.

Savory Pork Stir-Fry

MAKES 4 SERVINGS

1 pound lean boneless pork loin

1 tablespoon vinegar

1 tablespoon soy sauce

1 teaspoon sesame oil

1 clove garlic, minced

½ teaspoon ground ginger

1 teaspoon vegetable oil

1 (10-ounce) package frozen stir-fry vegetables, unthawed

1 tablespoon chicken broth or water

Hot cooked rice (optional)

1 tablespoon toasted sesame seeds (optional)

Slice pork across grain into ⅛-inch strips. Marinate in vinegar, soy sauce, sesame oil, garlic and ginger for 10 minutes. Heat vegetable oil in nonstick pan until hot. Add pork mixture and stir-fry for 3 to 5 minutes, until pork is no longer pink. Add vegetables and chicken broth. Stir mixture, cover and steam until vegetables are crisp-tender. Serve over hot cooked rice and sprinkle with toasted sesame seeds, if desired.

Favorite recipe from **National Pork Board**

Note:

Lean pork is a terrific source of protein, B vitamins and zinc. Loin and tenderloin are the leanest cuts of pork and adapt well to a wide variety of flavors and cooking methods.

Sesame-Garlic Flank Steak

MAKES 4 SERVINGS

1 beef flank steak (about 1¼ pounds)

2 tablespoons soy sauce

2 tablespoons hoisin sauce

1 tablespoon dark sesame oil

2 cloves garlic, minced

1. Score steak lightly with sharp knife in diamond pattern on both sides; place in large resealable food storage bag. Combine soy sauce, hoisin sauce, sesame oil and garlic in small bowl; pour over steak. Seal bag; turn to coat. Marinate in refrigerator at least 2 hours or up to 24 hours, turning once.

2. Prepare grill for direct cooking.

3. Drain steak, reserving marinade. Place on grid over medium heat. Grill, covered, 13 to 18 minutes for medium-rare (145°F) to medium (160°F) or until desired doneness, turning and brushing with marinade halfway through cooking time. Discard remaining marinade.

4. Transfer steak to cutting board; carve across the grain into thin slices.

Tip: When buying garlic, choose firm, dry heads of garlic with tightly closed cloves and smooth skin. Avoid garlic with sprouting green shoots. Store, unwrapped, in a cool, dry, dark place with good ventilation for 2 to 3 months.

FAR EAST
DESSERTS

Icy Mandarin Dessert
MAKES 10 SERVINGS

½ gallon vanilla frozen yogurt

¼ cup maple syrup

1 can (11 ounces) mandarin oranges, drained

½ cup halved seedless grapes

½ cup toasted pecans, broken into pieces

Additional chopped toasted pecans (optional)

1. Soften frozen yogurt until it resembles thick soup. Place in large loaf pan. Swirl in maple syrup. Fold in oranges, grapes and pecans. Freeze until firm.

2. Unmold onto cutting board. Slice and place onto plates when ready to serve. Garnish with pecans.

Ginger Spice Roll
MAKES 8 TO 10 SERVINGS

3 eggs, separated
½ cup (1 stick) butter, softened
½ cup light molasses
¼ cup granulated sugar
1 cup all-purpose flour
¾ teaspoon baking soda
½ teaspoon ground ginger
½ teaspoon ground cinnamon
½ teaspoon ground cloves
¼ teaspoon ground nutmeg
Powdered sugar
Spiced Filling (recipe follows)
Vanilla ice cream (optional)

1. Preheat oven to 375°F. Grease 15×10×1-inch jelly-roll pan. Line pan with parchment paper and grease; dust with flour.

2. Beat egg yolks 4 minutes in large bowl with electric mixer at high speed until mixture is thick and pale yellow. Add butter and molasses; beat 1 minute.

3. Beat egg whites in small bowl at high speed until foamy. Add granulated sugar, beating until soft peaks form. Fold into egg yolk mixture. Sift flour, baking soda, ginger, cinnamon, cloves and nutmeg into small bowl. Fold into egg mixture until well blended.

4. Pour batter into prepared pan. Bake 10 to 12 minutes or until cake is golden and edges begin to pull away from sides of pan.

5. Dust clean linen towel with powdered sugar. Invert cake onto towel. Peel off parchment paper; gently roll up cake with towel, starting from short side. Cool cake completely.

6. Prepare Spiced Filling.

7. Unroll cake; spread with Spiced Filling. Roll up cake; sprinkle with additional powdered sugar. Serve with vanilla ice cream, if desired.

Spiced Filling

1 package (8 ounces) cream cheese, softened
¼ cup (½ stick) butter, softened
½ teaspoon vanilla
1 cup powdered sugar
¼ teaspoon ground ginger
¼ teaspoon ground cinnamon

Beat cream cheese, butter and vanilla in medium bowl with electric mixer at medium speed until creamy. Beat in powdered sugar, ginger and cinnamon until smooth.

Almond Custard Cream Puffs

MAKES 8 SERVINGS

1 package (4-serving size) vanilla instant pudding and pie filling mix

1 cup cold milk

2 teaspoons almond-flavored liqueur or ½ teaspoon almond extract

1 cup whipped topping

¾ cup water

⅓ cup butter

¾ cup all-purpose flour

¼ teaspoon salt

3 eggs

1 can (11 ounces) mandarin orange segments, drained

Powdered sugar

1. For filling, beat pudding mix and milk in medium bowl with electric mixer at medium speed 2 minutes or until thickened. Stir in liqueur. Fold in whipped topping.

2. Cover with plastic wrap. Refrigerate until ready to fill cream puffs.

3. For cream puffs, preheat oven to 400°F. Grease baking sheet.

4. Bring water and butter to a boil in medium saucepan over high heat; stir until butter melts. Add flour and salt all at once, stirring vigorously. Continue cooking and stirring until mixture forms ball and pulls away from side of pan.

5. Remove from heat. Add eggs, one at a time, beating vigorously after each addition until mixture is smooth.

6. Drop heaping tablespoonfuls of batter into 8 mounds, 3 inches apart, onto prepared baking sheet.

7. Bake about 35 minutes or until puffed and golden brown. Cool slightly. Cut off tops and remove soft dough from insides. Cool completely on wire rack.

8. To serve, spoon filling into bottom of cream puffs. Place oranges on top of filling, then cover with tops. Dust cream puffs with powdered sugar.

Honey-Ginger Bourbon Balls
MAKES ABOUT 4 DOZEN BALLS

1 cup gingersnap cookie crumbs

1¼ cups powdered sugar, divided

1 cup finely chopped pecans or walnuts

1 square (1 ounce) unsweetened chocolate

1½ tablespoons honey

¼ cup bourbon

1. Combine crumbs, 1 cup powdered sugar and pecans in large bowl.

2. Combine chocolate and honey in top of double boiler over low heat; stir until chocolate is melted. Blend in bourbon.

3. Stir bourbon mixture into crumb mixture until well blended. Shape into 1-inch balls; roll in remaining ¼ cup powdered sugar. Refrigerate until firm.

Note:

Bourbon balls improve with age. Store them in an airtight container in the refrigerator. They will keep several weeks, but are best after two to three days.

Grilled Ginger Fruit

MAKES 6 SERVINGS

2 large ripe mangos, papayas or peaches

2 to 3 large ripe plums, halved and pitted

24 sweet cherries, halved and pitted

½ cup brandy

6 tablespoons sugar

2 tablespoons chopped crystallized ginger

1 tablespoon fresh lemon juice

2 teaspoons cornstarch

1 tablespoon orange- or cherry-flavored liqueur (optional)

Angel food cake (optional)

1. Spray 9-inch square foil baking pan with nonstick cooking spray; set aside. Peel mangos; slice pulp from pit and cut into ½-inch-wide slices. Place in prepared baking pan. Cut each plum half into 4 wedges; add to pan. Stir in cherries.

2. Combine brandy, sugar, ginger, lemon juice and cornstarch in small bowl. Stir until cornstarch dissolves; pour over fruit. Cover tightly with foil.

3. Prepare grill for direct cooking.

4. Place baking pan on grid over low heat. Grill, covered, 20 to 30 minutes or until juices simmer and fruit is tender. Stir in liqueur, if desired.

5. Spoon over cake, if desired, or serve in small bowls.

Note:

Firm fruits hold up best on the grill. Consider stirring in fresh berries after removing the grilled fruit from the heat and covering for a few minutes to warm through.

Chocolate Blaze
MAKES 16 SERVINGS

1 cup heavy cream

10 ounces semisweet chocolate chips*

2 tablespoons cold butter

¼ cup orange-flavored liqueur

Candied Orange Chips (recipe follows)

Pound cake or meringues

*Substitute bittersweet chocolate for a richer chocolate flavor.

1. Combine cream and chocolate chips in 10-inch skillet over low heat. Stir frequently until chocolate is melted. Remove from heat.

2. Add butter, stirring until well blended. Return to low heat. Pour liqueur into chocolate. Carefully ignite liqueur with long-handled lighter. Cook and stir until flames go out. Remove from heat.

3. Serve with Candied Orange Chips and pound cake or meringues.

Tip: Chocolate Blaze is also delicious over ice cream.

Candied Orange Chips

3 oranges

9 cups water

1 teaspoon salt

3 cups sugar

1. Using potato peeler, cut off peel into ½-inch wide strips (length of the orange itself.) Scrape inside of peel with paring knife to remove remaining white pith, if necessary.

2. Bring 3 cups of water to a boil in medium saucepan. Add peel and boil 5 minutes. Drain. Combine another 3 cups water and salt in same pan. Return to a boil. Add peel; reduce heat and simmer, uncovered, 5 minutes. Drain. Combine 3 cups water and 2 cups sugar in same saucepan. Bring to a boil. Add peel. Reduce heat and simmer 30 minutes or until peel is translucent. Let cool completely in syrup, about 1½ hours.

3. Drain peel. Place cooling rack on top of foil-lined sheet pan. Place remaining 1 cup sugar in shallow bowl. Coat peel in sugar; lay on rack. Let dry overnight. Store in airtight container at room temperature up to 1 week. Makes 36 to 40 chips.

Plum-Ginger Bruschetta

MAKES 9 SERVINGS

1 sheet frozen puff pastry (half of 17¼-ounce package)

3 plums, finely chopped (about 2 cups)

2 tablespoons sugar

2 tablespoons chopped candied ginger

1 tablespoon all-purpose flour

2 teaspoons lemon juice

⅛ teaspoon ground cinnamon

2 tablespoons apple jelly or apricot preserves

1. Unfold puff pastry and thaw 30 minutes on lightly floured work surface. Preheat oven to 400°F. Line baking sheet with parchment paper.

2. Cut puff pastry sheet lengthwise into 3 strips. Cut each strip crosswise in thirds to make 9 pieces. Place on prepared baking sheet. Bake 10 minutes or until puffed and lightly browned.

3. Meanwhile, combine plums, sugar, ginger, flour, lemon juice and cinnamon in medium bowl.

4. Gently brush each puff pastry piece with about ½ teaspoon jelly; top with scant ¼ cup plum mixture. Bake about 12 minutes or until fruit is tender.

Green Tea Lychee Frappé

MAKES 2 SERVINGS

1 can (15 ounces) lychees in syrup,* undrained

2 cups water

2 slices peeled fresh ginger (¼ inch thick, 2 inches wide)

3 green tea bags

*Canned lychees are readily available in either the canned fruit or ethnic foods section of most large supermarkets.

1. Drain lychees, reserving syrup. Place lychees in single layer in medium resealable food storage bag; freeze until frozen. Cover syrup; refrigerate.

2. Heat water and ginger in small saucepan over medium-high heat until water is boiling. Pour over tea bags in teapot or 2-cup heatproof measuring cup; steep 3 minutes. Discard ginger and tea bags. Cover tea; refrigerate until cool.

3. Place frozen lychees, chilled green tea and ½ cup reserved syrup in blender. Blend about 20 seconds until smooth. Serve immediately.

Note:

A lychee is a subtropical fruit grown in China, Mexico and the United States. It is a small oval fruit with a rough, bright red hull. Beneath the hull is milky white flesh surrounding a single seed. The flesh is sweet and juicy. The fresh lychee is a delicacy in China. They are available at Asian markets in the United States in early summer. Canned lychees are readily available. They are most often served as dessert.

*The publisher would like to thank the companies and organizations listed
below for the use of their recipes in this publication.*

ACH Food Companies, Inc.

Colorado Potato Administrative Committee

National Pork Board

Norseland, Inc.

METRIC CHART

VOLUME MEASUREMENTS (dry)

¹/₈ teaspoon = 0.5 mL
¹/₄ teaspoon = 1 mL
¹/₂ teaspoon = 2 mL
³/₄ teaspoon = 4 mL
1 teaspoon = 5 mL
1 tablespoon = 15 mL
2 tablespoons = 30 mL
¹/₄ cup = 60 mL
¹/₃ cup = 75 mL
¹/₂ cup = 125 mL
²/₃ cup = 150 mL
³/₄ cup = 175 mL
1 cup = 250 mL
2 cups = 1 pint = 500 mL
3 cups = 750 mL
4 cups = 1 quart = 1 L

VOLUME MEASUREMENTS (fluid)

1 fluid ounce (2 tablespoons) = 30 mL
4 fluid ounces (¹/₂ cup) = 125 mL
8 fluid ounces (1 cup) = 250 mL
12 fluid ounces (1¹/₂ cups) = 375 mL
16 fluid ounces (2 cups) = 500 mL

WEIGHTS (mass)

¹/₂ ounce = 15 g
1 ounce = 30 g
3 ounces = 90 g
4 ounces = 120 g
8 ounces = 225 g
10 ounces = 285 g
12 ounces = 360 g
16 ounces = 1 pound = 450 g

DIMENSIONS

¹/₁₆ inch = 2 mm
¹/₈ inch = 3 mm
¹/₄ inch = 6 mm
¹/₂ inch = 1.5 cm
³/₄ inch = 2 cm
1 inch = 2.5 cm

OVEN TEMPERATURES

250°F = 120°C
275°F = 140°C
300°F = 150°C
325°F = 160°C
350°F = 180°C
375°F = 190°C
400°F = 200°C
425°F = 220°C
450°F = 230°C

BAKING PAN SIZES

Utensil	Size in Inches/Quarts	Metric Volume	Size in Centimeters
Baking or	8×8×2	2 L	20×20×5
Cake Pan	9×9×2	2.5 L	23×23×5
(square or	12×8×2	3 L	30×20×5
rectangular)	13×9×2	3.5 L	33×23×5
Loaf Pan	8×4×3	1.5 L	20×10×7
	9×5×3	2 L	23×13×7
Round Layer	8×1½	1.2 L	20×4
Cake Pan	9×1½	1.5 L	23×4
Pie Plate	8×1¼	750 mL	20×3
	9×1¼	1 L	23×3
Baking Dish	1 quart	1 L	—
or Casserole	1½ quart	1.5 L	—
	2 quart	2 L	—